A Collection by David Miller

CB
CONTEMPORARY
BOOKS
CHICAGO

Library of Congress Cataloging-in-Publication Data

Miller, David, 1963–
    Dave / David Miller.
      p. cm.
    ISBN 0-8092-3626-5 (pbk.)
    1. Miller, David. 1963–   . 2. American wit and humor, Pictorial.
I. Title.
NC1429.M5377A4   1994
741.5'973—dc20   94-18885
                                           CIP

Published by Contemporary Books, Inc.
Two Prudential Plaza, Chicago, Illinois 60601-6790
Manufactured in the United States of America
International Standard Book Number: 0-8092-3626-5
10   9   8   7   6   5   4   3   2   1

4

5

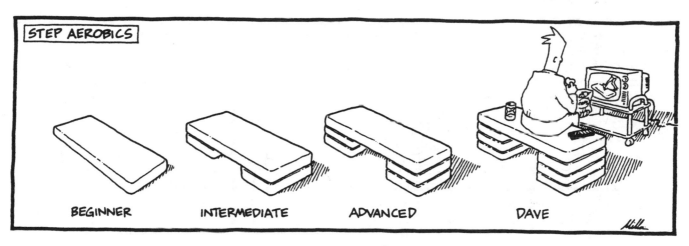

THE CLOSEST DAVE GETS TO REBELLION IS OCCASIONALLY RENTING "EASY RIDER"...

—AND IF I'M FEELING ESPECIALLY RECKLESS I WON'T EVEN REWIND IT!

I GOT THIS ONE IN 'NAM, THIS ONE IN NEW ORLEANS...

WOW!

COOL!

EXCUSE ME, I DON'T MEAN TO BRAG —BUT I GOT THIS ONE...

—IN THE MAIL ROOM!

DO NOT FOLD

WE ARE A '90's COUPLE —WE ARE NOT ADDICTED TO ANY SUBSTANCES...

—JUST EACH OTHER!

HIGH-LEVEL CORPORATE DECISION

DAVE-LEVEL DECISION

MMM... CHEESE PUFF-PUFFS!

YES, OFFICER, I WAS DRIVING IN THE CAR POOL LANE, BUT BEFORE YOU GIVE ME A TICKET, CONSIDER THIS...

CAR POOL L[?]
2 OR MORE PERS[?]
PER VEHICLE

—IN SOME THIRD WORLD COUNTRIES, I WOULD QUALIFY AS 2 OR MORE PERSONS!

DAVE!?

DAVE!?

WHAT!? GO AWAY! LEAVE ME **ALONE**!

LOOK, DARLA, I'M SORRY! I WAS CLEANING IT—AND IT ACCIDENTALLY WENT OFF!

19

20

21

THE CORPORATE CAREER PLAYGROUND

23

40

41

DAVE

BY DAVID MILLER

A MAN, HIS BEST FRIEND... AND HIS DOG!

CLICK CLICK click CLICK CLICK c CLICK CLICK click CLICK CLIC lick CLICK click CLICK clic CLICK click CLICK click CLICK c ICK click click CLICK CLICK lick click CLICK click CLICK k CLICK click click CLICK CLICK CLICK click CLICK CLICK CLI CLICK click click CLICK CLICK CLICK click click CLICK CL CLICK CLICK click CLICK click CLICK CL

A COLLEGE EDUCATION DOES NOT GUARANTEE A HIGH-PAYING, FAST-PACED CAREER!

CELEBRITIES AND ROCK STARS ARE PEOPLE - AND SHOULD NOT BE WORSHIPPED AS GODS!

CONSUMING A CERTAIN BRAND OF SOFT DRINK WILL NOT MAKE YOU A BETTER PERSON... ALTHOUGH STUDIES PROVE IT MAY QUENCH YOUR THIRST!

...AND HEY, WHO'S KIDDING WHO? YOUR TAXES WILL BE RAISED!

DAVE, WHAT ARE YOU WATCHING?

RTV.

OUR T.V.?

NO, DARLA, RTV!

REALITY T.V. - BECAUSE SOMEONE OWES YOU THE TRUTH!

DAVE AND DARLA RENEW THEIR MARRIAGE VOWS

YEAH... LIKE I DON'T HEAR ENOUGH VOICES IN MY HEAD ALREADY!

THE FIRST TIME YOU MISTAKENLY CALL YOUR GIRLFRIEND "MOM", IT'S CUTE...

HEE HEE, WHAT A SILLY MISTAKE.

-THE NEXT TIME IT QUALIFIES AS **FREUDIAN!**

I THINK DAVE'S BEEN WATCHING TOO MANY OF THOSE "REAL-LIFE" COP SHOWS!

DARLA... NEXT COMMERCIAL BREAK, COULD YOU MAKE US SOME POPCORN?

NEGOTIATION RULE #11.
ALWAYS BRING SOMETHING IMPRESSIVE TO THE BARGAINING TABLE.

SAY WHEN.

EXCUSE ME, WAITER... THERE MUST BE SOME MISTAKE!

DAVE AND THE LIGHTLY BROWNED CHUNKS OF TOFU

I KNOW, I KNOW, I MISS YOU TOO! BYE!

DAVE... WHO WAS THAT?

THE PIZZA GUY!

DAVE'S DIET - DAY FOUR

STOP 'N' GO

SUN 'N' FUN

STOP 'N' GO

OFFICE AUTOMATION

AUTO OFFICEMATION

I CAN ONLY HOPE THAT SOMEDAY I WILL HAVE ENOUGH MONEY TO SAY...

HEY! MONEY DOESN'T MATTER!

—AND REALLY MEAN IT !!!

MORE AMERICANS GET THEIR NEWS FROM:

A) NEWSPAPERS.

B) RADIO.

C) TELEVISION.

D) THAT KNOW-IT-ALL GUY AT BREAK TIME.

I'D JUST SAY LOOK, HILLARY, YOU TELL BILL...

WILL POWER

WON'T POWER

A BAD DAY

I COULD HAVE BEEN A FIREMAN!

A REALLY BAD DAY

I COULD HAVE BEEN A ROCKETTE!!!

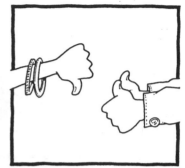

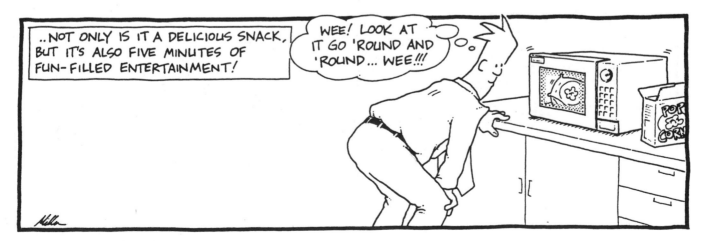

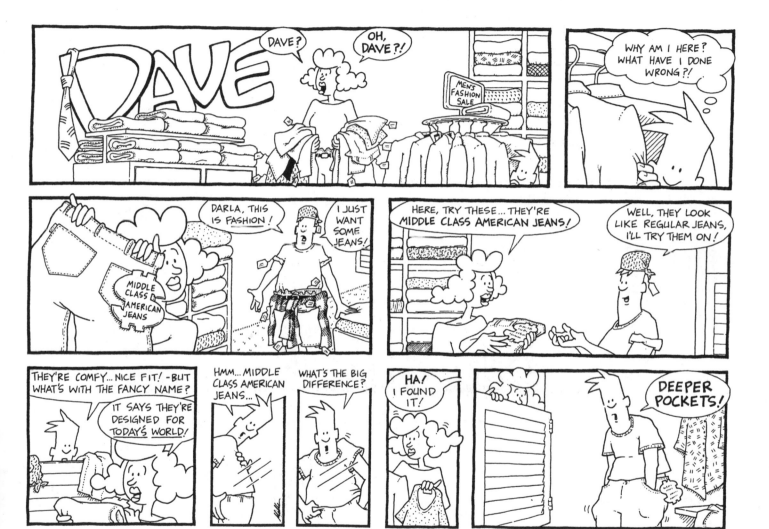

MORNING MEDITATION
NOT QUIT MY JOB TODAY... I WILL NOT
WILL NOT QUIT MY JOB TODAY... I WILL NOT
TODAY...I WILL NOT QUIT MY JOB TODAY...I
MY JOB TODAY... I WILL NOT QUIT MY
NOT QUIT MY JOB TODAY ...I WILL
LL NOT QUIT MY JOB TODAY...I
T MY JOB TODAY...I WILL NOT
B TODAY...I WILL NOT QUIT MY
QUIT MY JOB TODAY...I WILL
TODAY...I WILL NOT QUIT MY JOB
T MY JOB TODAY...I WILL NOT QUIT

DAVE &
DARLA
VISIT...

LA

DAY #1

DAVE &
DARLA
VISIT...

LA

DAY #2

DAVE &
DARLA
VISIT...

LA

DAY #3

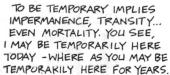

88

DAVE

BY DAVID MILLER

LOOK, DARLA, "SEE-THRU" COLA... IT'S NEW!!!

SPEC

CLEARLY A FAD!

HEY... NEWFANGLED ROUND TEA BAGS OR TRADITIONAL SQUARE ONES! IT'S A HOT BEVERAGE CONTROVERSY!

NEW

TURKEY HAM? TURKEY SAUSAGE? TURKEY BACON? WHERE ARE MY PORK PRODUCTS?

DARLA, HAVE YOU SEEN THIS? SHAMPOO AND CONDITIONER... IN ONE BOTTLE! LOOK!

I HAVE ONLY ONE QUESTION...

WHAT'S THAT, DAVE?

WHAT THE HECK IS CONDITIONER?!

DAVE

BY DAVID MILLER

EGO DRIVN
ALTERED STATE

DARLA, I'M THE MAN, I'M SUPPOSED TO DRIVE! MEN ARE SUPPOSED TO DRIVE. IT'S HORMONAL!

EVEN IF IT'S MY CAR?

MAD MAX

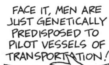

FACE IT, MEN ARE JUST GENETICALLY PREDISPOSED TO PILOT VESSELS OF TRANSPORTATION!

SPEED RACER

LOOK AT HISTORY... CHRISTOPHER COLUMBUS... NEIL ARMSTRONG... SANTA CLAUS... RICHARD PETTY... UM... KNIGHT RIDER... -ALL MEN!!!

OK! OK! STOP! YOU CAN DRIVE MY CAR!!!

JUST THINK OF ME AS STANDARD EQUIPMENT!

I DO, DAVE!

EVEL KNIEVEL

YOU'RE MY DRIVER-SIDE AIR HEAD!

100

DAVE... TREE-HUGGIN' ENVIRONMENTALIST —OR JUST ANOTHER LABOR DAY SOFTBALL BLOOPER?

THE MOST DIFFICULT ASPECT OF A HOLIDAY WEEKEND IS KNOWING JUST WHEN TO COME BACK!

THREE WAYS TO AVOID HARMFUL RADIATION EMITTED FROM YOUR PERSONAL COMPUTER

ONE!

TWO!

THREE!

DAVE

BY DAVID MILLER

DAVE, OUR CONSTANT ARGUING OVER "WHO GETS TO HOLD THE REMOTE CONTROL UNIT," IS REALLY ABOUT SOMETHING MUCH BIGGER !!!

YEAH, IT'S ABOUT THE T.V. !!!

MANY COUPLES COME TO ME FOR RELATIONSHIP COUNSELING...

—IN MOST INSTANCES, IT'S SIMPLY A MATTER OF IMPROVING COMMUNICATION SKILLS!

IT TAKES COURAGE TO SEEK PROFESSIONAL HELP, I APPLAUD YOUR EFFORTS!

WELL, DAVE DIDN'T WANT TO COME HERE, HE THINKS THIS IS SILLY... I JUST THINK HE'S FRIGHTENED!

NO, I'M NOT! DON'T SAY THAT!

WOW! HAVE YOU EVER WOKEN UP BEFORE YOUR ALARM GOES OFF?

I WONDER WHAT THAT'S LIKE?!

I'D COMPLAIN ABOUT THE TRAFFIC, -BUT I'M PART OF THE PROBLEM!!!

VARIOUS OFFICE TIES

THE "I CAN'T LET MY TIE GET IN THE WAY OF MY WORK" LOOK.

THE "I'M STARVED FOR ATTENTION - NOVELTY TIE " LOOK.

OH LOOK! IT'S BART!

THE "ASK ME ABOUT MY RECENT TRIP TO THE SOUTHWEST" LOOK.

THE "MY BRAIN NEEDS LESS BLOOD FLOW THAN YOUR BRAIN" LOOK.

THE "LAND A SMALL AIRCRAFT ON MY TIE " LOOK.

THINGS DAVE MAY NEVER ATTAIN:

A MOUSTACHE...

A GOOD CREDIT RATING

A BASIC UNDERSTANDING OF WOMEN

WHAT ABOUT ME?! DON'T I GET A TIME OF THE MONTH TOO?!

BEER!

DIET SODA!

PRETZELS!

CARROT STICKS!

EXPANSIVE T.V. LISTING!

EXTRA BATTERIES!

CLICK

WE'RE CABLE-READY!!!!

DARLA COMMUNICATES IN TERMS OF FEELINGS

A QUIET, ROMANTIC DINNER WITH POLITE, SENSITIVE CONVERSATION WOULD NOURISH MY HEART!

DAVE COMMUNICATES IN TERMS OF SYLLABLES

ME HUN·GRY!

DAVE

BY David Miller

YE OLD STOMPIN' GROUNDS RESTAURANT

DAVE, DID THE MENU GET STUCK TO YOUR FACE AGAIN?!

NO.

WELL, IS THIS SOME KIND OF "ZEN ORDERING THING"?! ARE YOU BECOMING "ONE" WITH THE MENU?!

NO.

IS IT TOO BRIGHT IN HERE?!

NO.

ARE YOU SMELLING THE MENU?!

NO.

DO YOU NEED GLASSES?!

NO.

I KNOW! IS THERE AN OLD GIRLFRIEND IN THE RESTAURANT?!

BINGO! -BUT PLEASE, DARLA, DON'T...

-MAKE A SCENE!

WHERE?! WHERE IS SHE?!

THE GENERATION X
PRENUPTIAL AGREEMENT
O.K., WHEN WE GET MARRIED AND WE DON'T END UP GETTING ALL THE NEAT STUFF THE GENERATION BEFORE US GOT, WE HEREBY AGREE THAT WE WILL NOT TURN OUR FRUSTRATIONS TOWARD EACH OTHER...BUT IN UNISON WE WILL TURN OUR FRUSTRATIONS TOWARD PREVIOUS PRESIDENTIAL ICONS AND THEIR CORRESPONDING POLICIES... —AND THEN... THEN WE'LL JUST WATCH SOME MORE T.V.!

DAVE AND HIS SIGNIFICANT OTTER

YOU'RE SPECIAL TO ME!

ZOO

DAVE, YOU'RE PUSHING MY BUTTONS AGAIN!

NO, NO, DARLA! YOU JUST CAN'T ACCEPT THE TRUTH!

YOU'RE LAZY!

YOU'RE CONTROLLING!

COME ON... YOU GET IT... —YOU'RE CLOSER!!!

FRISBEE

DAVE

BY DAVID MILLER

2-LATE

DAVE, YOU LOOK TERRIBLE! ARE YOU O.K.?!

I DIDN'T GET MUCH SLEEP! THE COLLEGE STUDENTS NEXT DOOR HAD AN ALL-NIGHT HOUSE PARTY!

SEPT.

THERE THEY GATHERED... "GRUNGE" CLAD AND SELF-ABSORBED...

OUR "HOPE OF THE FUTURE"...

"TOMORROW'S LEADERS."

-NOT YET TAINTED BY THE "TRY-AND-FIND-A-JOB" POST COLLEGE REALITY.

SWEATY, PIERCED AND OCCASIONALLY TATOOED, THE COLLEGE BOUND PULSED TO A DRONING NOISE.

HOURS PASSED AND THE CROWD OVER-FLOWED INTO THE SUBURBAN NIGHT: PILLAGING THE SANCTITY OF MY QUIET BEDROOM.

DID YOU CALL THE POLICE?

SEPT

I HAD NO CHOICE! THEY WOULDN'T LET ME IN!

DAVE SLEEPS THROUGH THE "AMERICAN DREAM"

LUCKY RECIPIENT
10 MILLION
$10,000,000
DOLLARS

KNOCK KNOCK

I GUESS HE'S NOT HOME... LET'S GO NEXT DOOR.

WARNING: USE OF THIS MINI-SPARE CAN RESULT IN SERIOUS INJURY TO THE MALE EGO.

I MIGHT AS WELL SPRAY PAINT "DORK" ON THE SIDE OF MY CAR !!!

PROFOUND MOMENTS OF SELF-REALIZATION

PRINCIPAL'S OFFICE

HMM... I MAY NEVER BECOME THE PRESIDENT OF THE UNITED STATES OF AMERICA !

HMM... I MAY NEVER BE FABULOUSLY WEALTHY !

LOTTER

Dave

BY David Miller

NETWORK RECIPES
IT'S EASY TO FEED THE MASSES

O.K., HERE'S THE RECIPE...

- START W/ A WELL-SEASONED TALKING HEAD
- ADD 2 MEATY, FRESH SOCIAL ISSUES
- CRACK OPEN A JUICY SCANDAL
- BLEND W/ A PROBING EXPOSÉ
- PERSEVERE W/ A DASH OF HOPE
- SPRINKLE WITH COMMERCIALS (OVER)

...DON'T FORGET TO LINE THE PAN WITH A SLICK CELEBRITY INTERVIEW; FINALLY TOP WITH SOME PACKAGED SINCERITY AND JUST A PINCH OF AUDIENCE BONDING!

PREHEAT OVEN, BAKE FOR 60 MINUTES...

30 MINUTES LATER... IT'S DONE!

BUT, DAVE... IT'S HALF-BAKED!

...YET ANOTHER HOUR MAGAZINE T.V. NEWS SHOW

IT SURE IS, DARLA!

DAVE

BY DAVID MILLER

NECESSITY, THE MOTHER OF INVENTION, PRESENTS THE "JUST CHECKIN' MIRROR"

HEY, DARLA, AM I STARTING TO GET "THIN" ON TOP?!

HMM...DO YOU WANT THE TRUTH...OR SOMETHING THAT WOULD MAKE YOU FEEL BETTER?!

-SOMETHING THAT WOULD MAKE ME FEEL BETTER!

O.K.

...HERE!

WOW! A DUCK-BILLED YUPPIE HAT!!!

O.K., NOW GIVE ME THE TRUTH!!!

140